ELIZABETH CADY STANTON

Library of Congress Number: 87-35585

Library of Congress Cataloging in Publication Data

Gleiter, Jan, 1947-
   Elizabeth Cady Stanton.

   (Raintree stories)
   Summary: A biography of one of the first leaders
of the women's rights movement, whose work led
to the adoption of the nineteenth amendment—
women's right to vote.
   1. Stanton, Elizabeth Cady, 1815-1902—Juvenile
literature.   2. Feminists—United States—Biography—
—Juvenile literature.   [1. Stanton, Elizabeth Cady,
1815-1902.   2. Feminists.]   I. Thompson, Kathleen.
II. Title.
HQ1413.S67G44   1988   305.4'2'0924   [B]   [92]   87-35585
ISBN 0-8172-2677-X (lib. bdg.)
ISBN 0-8172-2681-8 (softcover)

ELIZABETH CADY STANTON

Jan Gleiter and Kathleen Thompson

Illustrated by Rick Whipple

Raintree Childrens Books
Milwaukee

The year is 1854.

In one small town, a woman of twenty-seven tells her parents that she's going to visit her cousin. Actually, she isn't, and she hopes that her cousin will keep her promise to lie for her. She gets on the train for Albany.

In another town, a young wife hears her husband tell her that if she leaves, she should never come back. She gets into a carriage, believing that he loves her enough to change his mind, and sets out for Albany.

In a city, an old seamstress walks proudly toward the train station with a small sum of money clutched in her hand. She has saved every penny from her small wages for months. There will be nothing left for food after she buys her train ticket, but she is going to Albany.

At the end of their journey, these women and many others will gather together. There they will wait while another brave woman stands before a committee of lawmakers and says what is on her mind—and theirs. That woman is Elizabeth Cady Stanton.

Elizabeth was always a fireball. It was clear very early that she'd been given more than her share of energy, intelligence, and curiosity. The combination of these traits made Elizabeth unusual—especially for a young girl in the early nineteenth century.

But the real turning point in her young life came when her brother Eleazur was killed in a carriage accident. Elizabeth's father had always made it so plain that he loved his son better than his daughters! Now his son was dead.

Lizzie came up with a plan to comfort her father in his grief. She would learn the things that boys knew. She would ride and jump horses, climb trees . . . and learn Greek. She would try to take the place of a son in her father's heart.

Her first step was to surprise him with her knowledge of Greek. She went to her minister, Dr. Hosack, and asked him to teach her. When she told him her reason, he agreed, and they set to work at once. It wasn't long before Lizzie's extraordinary intelligence made Dr. Hosack decide to let her father in on the secret early.

The next thing Lizzie knew, her father had enrolled her in the Johnstown Academy. It was a school for boys. But the academy had just started allowing girls to take certain classes. Lizzie had never been happier.

All year she worked with one goal in mind—an award for her Greek studies. Her brother Eleazur had almost won the award when he was at the academy. She *would* win it.

And she did. At the end of the year, she rushed into her father's law office and showed him the beautiful Greek book with her name in gold letters. He looked at her with pride . . . and with sadness.

"You should have been a boy," he said.

She almost believed him. Life would be a lot easier if she were a boy. All the things she wanted would be hers. But underneath it all, Elizabeth Cady liked being Elizabeth Cady. She didn't want to be a boy. She just wanted being a girl to be different.

After she won the prize for her Greek studies, Elizabeth was allowed to spend some time in her father's law office. She would curl up in a chair and read his laws books. At first, they seemed as hard as Greek. But gradually, Elizabeth began to understand them.

What she understood, she didn't like. Some of the laws in the books were so unfair to women that she found it hard to believe they were real. Then there were the women who came into her father's office. Some of them told stories that made Elizabeth hot with anger. One of those women was Mrs. MacPherson.

Mrs. MacPherson had relatives in Scotland. One of them had died and left her some money. Her husband lost almost all of it on foolish schemes before he died. Now, her son wanted to take the rest of it and put her out of her own house. What could she do?

"Nothing," said Mr. Cady sadly. A married woman, under the law, could not own anything. Her money and her house had belonged to her husband. Now they belonged to her son. There was absolutely nothing she could do.

Elizabeth would never forget Mrs. MacPherson.

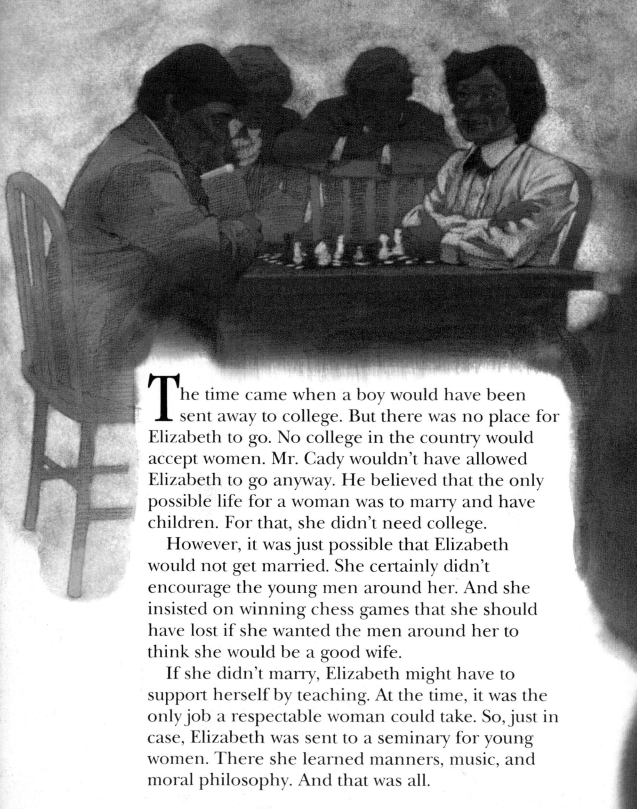

The time came when a boy would have been
sent away to college. But there was no place for
Elizabeth to go. No college in the country would
accept women. Mr. Cady wouldn't have allowed
Elizabeth to go anyway. He believed that the only
possible life for a woman was to marry and have
children. For that, she didn't need college.

However, it was just possible that Elizabeth
would not get married. She certainly didn't
encourage the young men around her. And she
insisted on winning chess games that she should
have lost if she wanted the men around her to
think she would be a good wife.

If she didn't marry, Elizabeth might have to
support herself by teaching. At the time, it was the
only job a respectable woman could take. So, just in
case, Elizabeth was sent to a seminary for young
women. There she learned manners, music, and
moral philosophy. And that was all.

Elizabeth's life changed again several years later when she met Henry Stanton. In her heart, Elizabeth had sworn she would never marry because it meant giving up all her rights. But Henry Stanton changed her mind. He was a passionate crusader against slavery and all forms of injustice. He believed, as Elizabeth did, that the laws against women's rights were wrong. And, since Elizabeth also happened to be very much in love with him, she agreed to marry him.

That was the beginning of Elizabeth Cady Stanton's work in the antislavery movement. That work eventually led her to fight for the rights of women.

At an abolitionist convention in London, Elizabeth met the Quaker woman Lucretia Mott, a leader in the fight against slavery. The two women, along with all the other women delegates, sat behind a curtain so that they could hear what was said at the convention. They were not allowed to talk. They were not even allowed to watch or to be seen. And this was a convention of men who were dedicating their whole lives to fighting injustice!

Elizabeth and Lucretia decided then and there that they would hold a convention of women someday to begin the fight for women's rights.

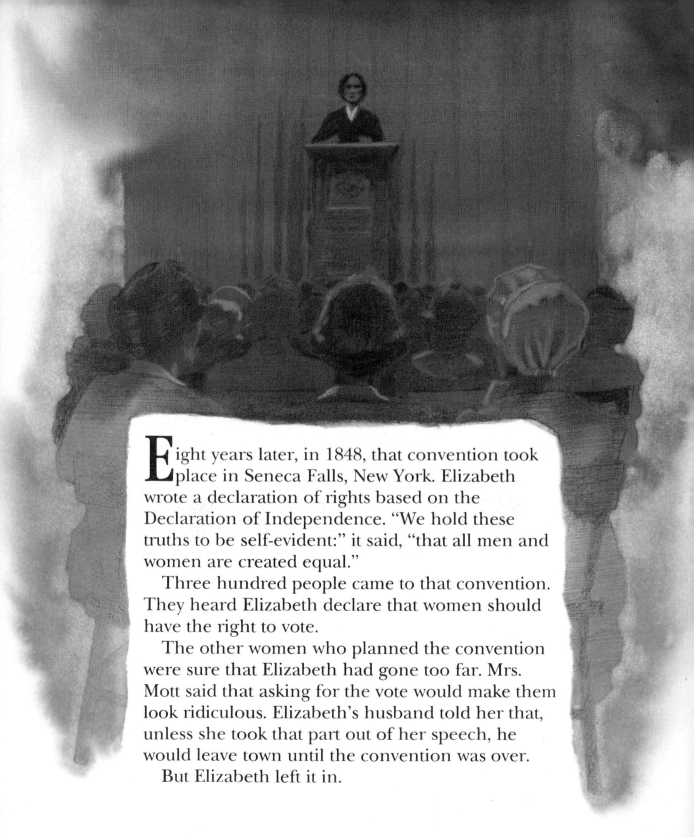

Eight years later, in 1848, that convention took place in Seneca Falls, New York. Elizabeth wrote a declaration of rights based on the Declaration of Independence. "We hold these truths to be self-evident:" it said, "that all men and women are created equal."

Three hundred people came to that convention. They heard Elizabeth declare that women should have the right to vote.

The other women who planned the convention were sure that Elizabeth had gone too far. Mrs. Mott said that asking for the vote would make them look ridiculous. Elizabeth's husband told her that, unless she took that part out of her speech, he would leave town until the convention was over.

But Elizabeth left it in.

25

Two years after that convention, Elizabeth Cady Stanton met Susan B. Anthony. The two women formed a partnership that would make history.

Elizabeth, at home with her many children, wrote the words. Susan went out on the road, organizing and speaking. She talked to shop girls and society women. She spoke to groups of two and to groups of two hundred. And always, Susan went back to Elizabeth for more words.

"You stir up Susan," said Henry Stanton to his wife, "and she stirs up the world."

But a day came when Elizabeth went out to
speak her own words. It was time, she decided,
for the legislators in her state to change some of
those laws she first learned about in her father's
office. It was time for them to protect the Mrs.
MacPhersons of the world.

A group of lawmakers agreed to listen to her. At
once, Susan started organizing. While Elizabeth
spoke to the men, women from all over the state
and the country would gather in Albany to support
her. Petitions would be circulated so that people
who could not come to the convention could be
heard. Elizabeth would have their strength to add
to the strength of her own words and ideas.

They all came—the women, the girls, the wives, the teachers. It was 1854, and women did not travel alone, but these women did. They came by train, in carriages, and on foot. They were women Susan had talked to using Elizabeth's words. They were women who wanted to be free.

When the committee of men reported back to the legislature, it was clear that the women had lost. The lawmakers recommended that no action be taken. But they did suggest that the men who had signed the women's petitions should take up wearing skirts.

It wasn't Elizabeth's first loss. It wouldn't be her last one. But there would be victories, too, in the fifty years that Elizabeth and Susan worked together for freedom. Finally, just eighteen years after Elizabeth died in 1902, women would finally have the right to vote.

But fifty years after Elizabeth Cady Stanton's death, there were still states where married women could not own property in their own names. Seventy-five years later, there were still states where a man could have his wife committed to a mental institution on his word alone.

Today, the amendment to the Constitution guaranteeing equal rights for women has still not passed.